MW01627034

Illustrated by

Max Elbo

 Printed in the United States of America. For more information, write:

BSC, Inc. Publications
2522 Highland Avenue
Cincinnati OH 45219
(513) 221-8545

ISBN 0-938837-02-8

For "The Little Girl"

For Each Part of Every One

The Discoveries of Separateness
Adventures of Oneness

To My Parents, Nettie & Dave Adams

Once there was a little girl who lived in a cold and rainy country where the sun hardly shone. This child had been hurt by many people and had not been taken care of very well. It seemed that she was always cold and hungry. The little girl didn't feel loved; in fact, in the depths of her heart, she felt all alone.

During very hard times the little girl comforted herself by dreaming, especially daydreaming. She would often smile at the thought of running away to a warm and sunny land where people were nice and food was plentiful. One day while she was dreaming, daydreaming that is, the little girl decided to make one of her dreams come true. She decided to go away.

The little girl packed some apples, nuts and biscuits, looked hard and long at her country and family, and was saddened that her life had been so painful. She took a deep breath and then set her feet on a path which led to the sea. There, she knew, just as she sometimes sensed things in her daydreams, that she would be able to get a ride across the ocean to a warm, sunny and friendly land.

The path which led to the sea went through a large and dark forest, which the little girl had heard was filled with unfriendly animals. At the entrance to the forest, the little girl sat at the foot of a large tree and cried. As badly as she wanted to follow the path to the sea so that she could find a warm and sunny place to live, she was fearful.

As she sat crying under the tree, the little girl heard a very soft voice. "Little Girl, why are you crying?" The child looked up shyly and saw next to her a beautiful lady dressed in blue light. The lady seemed to be floating, for her feet did not quite touch the ground.

While the little girl was surprised to see such a sight, she knew somehow that the lady was not a total stranger. There was something very familiar about the lady. The child responded, "I am crying because I am sad and fearful. I was hurt over and over again in the land where I lived." She paused, took a deep breath, and looked at the lady. It was not easy for the little girl to speak of painful matters. She had never told anyone these secrets. The lady, who seemed to understand, smiled warmly and with a slow gesture of her hand encouraged the little girl to continue her story. The child swallowed back her tears and went on.

I am going across the sea to find a place to live where the sun shines and the people are friendly. But, as you can see for yourself, first I must go through this awful forest. This forest," gulped the little girl, "is full of dangerous animals."

The lady smiled and said, "I know all of which you speak. I am going to help you get through the forest to the sea, where, as you already know, there will be awaiting a marvelous ride to warm and friendly places. I could just whisk you there myself, but I and all of the wise people who love you from afar want to see you grow strong. Then you will be able to take care of yourself and be happy." Moving gently within the blue light, the lady continued, "During the journey through the forest, you will acquire much wisdom. Wisdom helps you know what is good and true. It is a treasure which will assist you forever and ever."

The little girl, who was very tired, asked the lady in blue light, "Couldn't you just whisk me there right away?" The lady smiled softly, wrapped her blue light around the little girl, and helped her drift into a deep and restful sleep. The lady then sang gently to the child. She sang of warm and friendly places.

When the little girl awakened, she was fresh and felt very brave. She decided to do as the lady had suggested so that she could grow strong, wise and happy. The lady, pleased with the little girl's decision, continued, "I am a part of you, and I will always be with you. Any time you wish, you may wrap up in this light and rest. If you do get fearful, close your eyes, have your mind reach deep within, wish for the first thing that comes to mind, and then clap your hands."

"Now listen very carefully," said the lady. "You must think of what you want rather than what you fear. Repeat this, please, for the phrase is very important." The little girl took a deep breath, stood exceptionally straight, and said, "I must think of what I want rather than what I fear." The little girl gave the lady a warm hug, wrapped up in the blue light, picked up her apples, nuts and biscuits, and set off straight into the forest.

At first the forest felt friendly. The child could hear little birds chirping in the trees, and the ground made funny noises as she went along her way. She was somewhat frightened, but she kept thinking of the bright and sunny land where the people were friendly. She also thought of the mysterious lady who promised to help her through this difficult journey.

The deeper the little girl went into the woods, the darker it became. A soft blue glow lighted the path for her. Nevertheless, after some time in the dark, the child began hearing strange and scary noises. The girl became very frightened. "What am I going to do?" she thought. The words which the lady had spoken came back to her: "You must think of what you want rather than what you fear."

Instead of thinking of the animals and the harm they might do her, the little girl did what the lady in blue light had suggested. First she closed her eyes. The child allowed her mind to travel deep within and rest for a while. She thought, "I wish there were someone with me so that I wouldn't have to face this trip all by myself." Satisfied with her wish, the little girl clapped her hands. Slowly opening her eyes, the little girl saw that next to her was another child who was bright and alert and not fearful at all. They laughed. Together they were braver and stronger. The two little girls made a tiny fire, curled up in the warmth of its glow, told each other stories, and fell asleep in the midst of the noises of the forest. Above them was a soft and smiling blue light.

Having rested well, the two children set out early the next morning. Suddenly they heard a loud roar. The children stopped and huddled together. Closing their eyes, both children allowed their minds to quiet and go deep within. They wished and clapped their little hands. As they slowly opened their eyes, each beheld the amazing sight of more and more children of all sizes and shapes, all ready to make the journey through the woods together.

The children joined each other, singing and pushing through the woods. They grew quiet, however, as soon as they heard the noises of fierce-sounding animals. They heard them shout that they were looking for little children to devour. All of the youngsters hid. When the forest again became quiet, the children got together and talked. One child said, "Some of us will have to be very tough if we are to handle the monsters of the forest." To this end several of the children grew to enormous sizes and became very stern-looking, so much so that they frightened each other.

Other children developed different special talents. Some children became experts at hiding; some learned to run very fast; others never said a word and were able to be very quiet. Certain children learned to find and cook food, while others became cheerful and entertained the little troupe.

The group of clever and strong children went through the woods putting off some of the wildest creatures. Everyone had tasks to do. Each child was equally important. Each needed the other. Working together the children were very effective. They were so effective, in fact, that when the animals saw what they called "the herd of children" coming, they ran the other way. The children were jubilant as they marched on their way to the sea.

As sometimes happens in life, some of the children forgot or became distracted from their goal of reaching the warm and sunny land. Some of them, in the excitement of their very special talents or skills, began to think that they were more important than the others. One would brag, "I am the most necessary, for I am the strongest." Another would say, "If I didn't cook the food, none of you could do anything. I am the best." Several of the children began to scare or trick the others. Some became very self-centered and thought only of themselves. Others became very critical.

The situation was certainly getting out of hand. Many of the youngsters became frightened of the others and even of themselves. Some withdrew. The little troupe of children went forward, but they were not very happy. The blue light shone, but was not as bright.

One day the worried children heard a most ferocious sound, the bellowing of the Big Dragon. All became frightened and gathered together again. The youngsters had to put aside their differences and work together on this one, or they might all be killed. As the children shivered, a voice was heard: "Remember to think of what you want rather than what you fear." The children quietly made a circle, closed their eyes, traveled deep within, and wished for a plan. The blue light became brighter and brighter.

The troupe marched on bravely. When they heard the dragon coming, the children made a large circle around the path and hid behind the rocks, trees, and bushes. When the dragon came to the path, all the children bravely played their parts. Just as if they were singing in time with one another, each child in turn called to the dragon. "Hey, you!," "Dragon!," "Firemouth!," "Over here!" were just some of the cries.

The baffled creature turned to find the child behind each voice, but the children were hidden. As the cries went on, the Big Dragon continued to wheel, first to one voice, then to the next. Before long the dragon was very dizzy and didn't quite know where he stood. He bellowed with frustration, but only put forth a feeble flame. At this point all the children came out and told off the dragon: "Why don't you become a vegetarian?!" "Pick on somebody your own size!" "You are such a bully!" "Go away and leave us alone!" The Big Dragon, who by this time was very confused, dizzily slunk away, vowing to himself never to fool with children again.

Being very proud of themselves, the children triumphantly resumed their journey. The woods were dark, but the children could tell when they were getting close to the sea. Beyond the darkness, a clearing could be seen. All the children broke into a run. They ran to the clearing, through the sand, and into the water. For miles around the sounds of laughter, songs and splashing could be heard.

Out of the mist at the edge of the sea appeared a magical white swan. The swan was pulling a silver boat which was covered with a glimmering light. Alongside the sea was the lady. "Children," she said, "this is the boat that will take you to the land where the sun shines and the people are friendly. But first you have to make one more wise plan. For you see, the little boat will hold only one child."

The shocked children looked at each other. Each child thought, "What if I don't get to go?" Spreading the blue light over the children, the lady said, "Remember to think of what you want, not what you fear." The children became peaceful and began thinking the same thoughts. They realized that in spite of their differences what they all wanted more than anything else was to go to the warm and sunny land. In their wisdom, the children were able to quietly place this new fear aside.

The children began recounting all of their adventures, working backwards from the dragon. They remembered how each child had come to be. The children recalled that they all had come from the one little girl. They became separate because of a need for survival and learning. That need no longer existed; in fact, the separateness was creating a problem.

Again the little group made a circle, closed their eyes, and went deep within. Each child's wish was clear. As the many hands clapped enthusiastically, the blue light swirled around and around. Soon the light lifted, and the radiant little girl stood alone, her hair shimmering in the sunlight. "I am brave and strong and fast and clever," she said. "I was one person all along. For this adventure through the forest I needed to become many. At one point I almost worked against myself, but having to face the Big Dragon required all of me to work together in harmony. My wish to ride in the silver boat has made me one again. Now I am ready for my trip to the sunny land where the people are friendly."

The little girl quietly stepped into the silver boat. She no longer saw the lady in blue light, but she knew that she lived within her wise, strong self. The gentle swan turned, looked at her, and began softly swimming across the sea to the sunny land.

Most stories end by saying that "They all lived happily ever after," but that isn't the way life really is. The truth is that the little girl, who had grown strong and wise, was off for more adventures. She would be forever growing stronger and wiser. The child's many adventures would teach her more and more about the nature of life. With each experience her light would become brighter and brighter.

The End

About the Author

ANN ADAMS, R.N.P., M. N. Sc.,

is a Registered Nurse Practicioner in private practice in Eureka Springs, Arkansas. She is also employed at St. John's Adolescent Treatment Center and the Shealy Institute, both in Springfield, Missouri. She has a Masters Degree in Mental Health Nursing from the University of Arkansas for the Medical Sciences.

In addition to **The Silver Boat**, Ms. Adams has authored chapters in **Mental Health - Psychiatric Nursing**, and **Clinical Manual of Psychiatric Nursing**, and has written "*Internal Self Helpers of Persons with Multiple Personality Disorder*", an article for the **Journal of Dissociation**. Recently she has presented papers at the annual conference of the International Society for the Study of Multiple Personality and Dissociation (1987, 1988, 1989, and 1990).

About the Artist

MAX ELBO

is a self-taught graphic artist who lives in Eureka Springs, Arkansas. He began his career designing posters in the late 60's. He does commercial art for local businesses as well as private commissions and portraits. The pictures in this book are pen and ink drawings colored with markers. This is Max Elbo's first illustrated children's book.